ABC

What Can You Grow Up to Be?

By Josée Lavoie

*To Mom & Dad, who always
encouraged me to chase my dreams.*

ABC What Can You Grow Up to Be?
© Text by Josée Lavoie. 2022
© Illustrations by Josée Lavoie. 2022

Published by Josée Lavoie

HeyJosee.com

ISBN:
978-1-7781934-0-8 (Paperback)
978-1-7781934-5-3 (Hardcover)
978-1-7781934-4-6 (eBook)

First Edition, 2022

When you grow up, you can become a dentist, a mail carrier or even an athlete!

Learn the letters from

A to Z

and discover what you could be!

Aa

Ammar is an artist.

Bb

Béatrice is a ballerina.

Cc

Charlie is a chef.

Dd

David is a detective.

Ee

Elena is an electrician.

Ff

Félix is a florist.

Gg

Gloria is a guitarist.

Hh

Hugo is a hockey player.

Ii

Imani is an interpreter.

Jj

Joey is a juggler.

Kk

Kayla is a karateka.

Léo is a linguist.

Mm

Meilin is a mechanic.

Nn

Niko is a ninja.

Oo

Obi is an optician.

Pp

Penny is a pilot.

Qq

Quincy is a quarterback.

Rr

Rachel is a reporter.

Ss

Samuel is a superhero.

Tt

Tania is a therapist.

Uu

Uzuri is an urban planner.

Vv

Vanessa is a veterinarian.

Ww

Wilma is a web designer.

Xavier is an X-ray technician.

Yy

Youssef is a YouTuber.

Zz

Zoey is a zoologist.

Now you know the letters from A to Z

Did you discover what you could be?

Made in United States
North Haven, CT
30 June 2022

20822417R00020